Challenge

How governors can challenge school leaders effectively

David Marriott

Adamson Publishing Ltd

Copyright © David Marriott 2017

info@adamsonbooks.com
www.adamsonbooks.com

First published 2017

ISBN 978 0948543 54 8

British Library Cataloguing in Publication Data
A catalogue record for this book is available from the British Library

Cover design by Geoff Shirley

Printed by Short Run Press Ltd, Exeter

"When inspectors judge the leadership and management of a school to be less than good, a common underlying weakness is the failure of governors to hold school leaders to account."
Improving Governance: Governance arrangements in complex and challenging circumstances, Ofsted, 2016

"If your uncle is going in for brain surgery do you need someone going in from the community to oversee it? The principle *[of school governance]* is exactly the same. You are putting unpaid volunteers in the heart of a highly pressurised and extremely professional group of people. What the bloody hell for?"
Andrew Fielder, CEO, Aspire Academy Trust, Cornwall

"There are three sides to every story: yours ... mine ... and the truth. No one is lying."
Robert Evans, Hollywood film-maker

Contents

Introduction

The undefined words "challenge(s)" and "challenging" occur 13 times in the *Governance Handbook* and 37 times in the Ofsted *School Inspection Handbook*. The purpose of this book is to demystify and explore what "challenge" means for school and academy governors – and offer practical ways of carrying it out successfully

School governors – unpaid volunteers with (usually) no experience in education other than having been educated themselves – are expected to hold professional school leaders to account for standards and progress in their schools by challenging them on the basis of data and other evidence.

To any fair-minded observer this must seem a difficult, if not impossible task. It is not a contest of equals. The head who wants to minimise or deflect challenge has many options. The governor who seeks to challenge robustly faces formidable obstacles.

For Andrew Fielder, CEO, Aspire Academy Trust, Cornwall (an ex-headteacher) it makes no sense:

> "If your uncle is going in for brain surgery do you need someone going in from the community to oversee it? The principle *[of school governance]* is exactly the same. You are putting unpaid volunteers in the heart of a highly pressurised and extremely professional group of people. What the bloody hell for?"

According to the *i* newspaper (17/3/17) "The Aspire Academy Trust has taken the step to ditch governors in favour of advisory 'hubs', representing up to three academies. The trust sponsors 21 schools in Cornwall, but has done away with 'unpaid volunteers' in favour of 'professionals' appointed by the trust itself."

Is challenge an impossible task, then?

If it were, this book would not need to exist. How to challenge does, however, need examining. Going beyond paying lip service to "challenge" is this book's key focus. The emphasis is on the practical issues that arise from governors trying to carry out this role in real schools, with real headteachers – the human angle, to put it simply.

The main sections of the book are interspersed with vignettes in the form of play scripts capturing conversations between heads and governors which exemplify some of the problems of offering challenge and being challenged. The vignettes are included to provoke questions and thought on the readers' part. Suggested ways forward in addressing the issues raised by each vignette are provided immediately afterwards.

There is a danger in thinking that challenge is solely concerned with asking questions based on an understanding of school performance data. While that is certainly vital, the book emphasises the fact that there are many areas of school life beyond what is captured on a spreadsheet or a scatter graph where challenge is necessary and appropriate, important though the data are.

The book also explores the challenge of challenge in a variety of school contexts, such as the small village school and the large multi-academy trust.

And in response to Andrew Fielder, I would argue that he is completely wrong.

His comments betray some underlying prejudices against and misunderstandings of school governance that this short book seeks to address.

First, school governors don't just represent the community and haven't done for the last decade. The emphasis in recent years has been on skills rather than representation. But then again, why should there not be a community presence in a local governing body? The school or academy exists to serve the community in which it sits, not some remote trust board.

Second, in his use of the phrase "unpaid volunteers" he implies that people paid to do the job would be better at it and that volunteers cannot also do a job in a professional manner. Both of these implied criticisms are demonstrably untrue. There are many national and international organisations that have paid governance but which have proved ineffective, otherwise we would not have seen the succession of failures that hit the headlines, not least the financial crash of 2008 and subsequent banking scandals, for example.

I do not suppose that if Mr Fielder were bleeding to death and being attended to by a member of the St John's Ambulance Brigade he would prefer to die than have his life saved by this unpaid volunteer.

Many school governors come from a wide range of professional backgrounds and understand the need to behave professionally at least as well as those in institutions who are actually paid for doing the job. And it has to be said that the "extremely professional group of people" running the country's academies and academy chains have not always behaved as impeccably as Mr Fielder assumes.

In September 2016, for example, the principal of a flagship free school, Kings Science Academy in Bradford, was jailed for five years for his part in defrauding the government out of £69,000. The principal, his sister (also a teacher at the school), and the school's former financial director, were convicted by jury of a total of ten charges – including fraud, false accounting and acquiring criminal property. The free school was set up in 2010 by the principal and primarily run by him. During the trial the court heard that public money from grants given to the defendants by the Department of Education to set up the school and run it were treated "as their own" for over three years. An extreme and unusual example, it must be said – but it did happen.

There is also the important legal concept of the board of governors being a corporate body. It is the collective strength and knowledge of the board that matters. While school governance has its weaknesses and some school governors are more effective than others, one could say exactly the same about the professionals in charge of our schools, who, in contrast to school governors, are paid out of the public purse and should therefore be subject to public scrutiny and accountability. Trusting this job to "professionals appointed by the trust itself" is a dangerous step. External, objective scrutiny by disinterested members of the public has to be a better option. That is what school governance offers and achieves, at its best.

Background and context

The 1988 Education Reform Act reassigned the responsibility for schools' strategic planning and accountability from local education authorities to schools' governing bodies. Regulations published in 2000 stated that "The governing body shall act as 'critical friend' to the head teacher, that is to say, they shall support the head teacher in the performance of his functions and give him *[sic]* constructive criticism." A shift of emphasis and word order from "support and challenge" to "challenge and support" has been gradual but significant as the expectations of governance from the DfE and Ofsted have risen steadily this century.

To illustrate this trend, one might consider the foreword to the DfE's 2017 *Competency Framework for Governance*, written by Sir David Carter, National Schools Commissioner for England, which includes:

> "Governors or trustees who work as a team, who are able to bring their skills and experience to the role and who blend challenge and support to hold their workforce to account, will improve standards."

The longest section of the Competency Framework concerns "Accountability for educational standards and financial performance", broken down into six sub-sections, each detailing high expectations of the governing board, individual governors and the chair. A quick skim read of these expectations will confirm that the level of performance and range of skills and behaviours required bear all the characteristics of a high-powered and well-remunerated full-time professional job.

Vignette 1

CLEANING CONTRACT

CG: I wonder whether we shouldn't be looking to cancel the cleaning contract, if the cleaners really aren't leaving the school in a fit state?

CC: Well, it's only just under a year since we changed from Evans Cleaning ...

LA gov: That's not the point, though, is it? I mean, we pay for a service, there's a contract in place ... if the company can't or won't deliver, then of course we need to change provider.

CC: No, I wasn't suggesting we shouldn't change, just that we might struggle to find another provider in the area.

CG: Which providers do other schools use?

Head: It varies. A lot of schools used to use the LA service but became dissatisfied with it. The standards fell after it was contracted out. Then everyone did their own thing but I don't think anyone's found a firm they're totally happy with.

CG: Aren't we paying more now than we did to the LA?

Head: No – it's about the same and it is a better service overall, just not perfect.

CG: So is it a question of demanding even better service rather than changing provider again?

SBM: I could have another look at the contract, if you like and get back on to the manager to see if we can raise standards.

CG: What I don't really get is that the main cleaner is Janice, isn't it, and isn't she the kitchen manager as well? Can we sack her, or maybe do something through appraisal?

Head: I think that might be a bit of a blind alley. Janice has a 50 per cent

In all the vignettes CC = committee chair, CG = community governor, FG = foundation governor, LA gov = LA governor, PG = parent governor, SBM = school business manager, SG = staff governor and VC = vice chair.

contract with Bright Spark cleaning and her line manager for that work is Ken at Bright Spark. All I can do is appeal to him. I'm not Janice's line manager in that regard.

SBM: The other half of her time is as kitchen manager and we employ her directly for that work – but we're happy with the job she does.

LA gov: So the issue really is with Bright Spark, isn't it? Can't we just insist that this Ken person puts more pressure on Janice?

Head: We have tried and Ken always says he'll speak to her. To be fair, one of his co-managers did a review of the quality of cleaning and they said it was fine.

CG: And was it?

Head: Well, yes, on the day of the inspection, it was. I went round the school before the inspection and everything was fine, including the areas we're concerned about, like the hall and the boys' toilets. So I think the review was fair and we have the report. We looked at it last time, didn't we?

CG: Yes, we did. But clearly things aren't as good as they should be and I'm feeling frustrated that we …

Head: Well, so am I. I have spent a lot of time on this already and it's taking me away from the more important priorities, like the SATs. I do want the school to be as clean as possible but I feel that I'm not really getting anywhere.

CC: So, we sense that this is becoming a bit of a distraction for you. Is there a better way of dealing with it that would also take the responsibility off you?

Head: If only!

CC: Karen, is there anything else you could do, as School Business Manager?

SBM: I'd be happy to but I think we've tried most things now, so I'm not sure what else I could do.

CC: OK. So, first things first, then. I propose that we take the responsibility off the head, if everyone agrees?

Head: Well, I need to keep an eye on it, though …

CC: I'm not sure you do, with all due respect. We need you to focus on standards and progress, not the state of the toilets. It seems to be well within Karen's capabilities …

SBM: And it is in my JD …

LA gov: Oh, I'd forgotten that.

CC: Me too. So, if Karen takes responsibility, what are we saying she should do?

Head: Er … excuse me. I mean, I appreciate you taking the load off me but I'm Karen's line manager, so it should be me that decides what she does.

CC: I'm sorry. I do understand that and I'm sorry if I gave the impression of taking over your role. What I meant was, has anyone got any suggestions as to a way forward that the head could consider, then ask Karen to get on with?

CG: How about Karen doing a quick phone around to find out what other

11

schools are doing – who's good and reasonably priced and so on, then sharing that with the committee so we can recommend a new supplier?

CC: OK. It's probably worth another shot. In the meantime, Karen, could you also take a wider look at cleaning contractors? They don't necessarily need to be based in our area, do they? Inviting a new competitor in might shake up some of the companies we've used before – get them to raise their game.

SBM: What if we suggest this approach to at least some of the other schools in the area? If we all changed provider at the same time, it would send out a powerful message and increase our buying power.

CC: Great idea! Are you happy to put out some feelers and report back?

SBM: Yes, that's fine. When would you like the information?

CC: When do we meet next? How about putting it on GovernorHub so we can all have a look before the next meeting, then we can decide quickly?

Head: That does sound like a positive way forward.

COMMENTARY

This vignette sees governors working well together as a team in order to achieve a positive outcome.

All schools can choose their service suppliers but academies tend to be more proactive in this respect. Cleaning contracts are often difficult to get right. The cheapest provider is seldom the best but finding a conscientious cleaning team at a reasonable charge can be difficult.

A clean school is a basic requirement. The headteacher knows the history and seems frustrated with the fact that it seems well-nigh impossible to find a reliable firm. It sounds as though she has spent an inordinate amount of time trying to resolve the matter, with little success. She seems to be under stress, though it's partly self-created, possibly through an unrealistic desire to micromanage everything.

The challenge offered by the governors is to the head's reluctance to delegate responsibility.

The School Business Manager appears to be an under-used resource in this regard. The headteacher seems to be taking on too much responsibility when the SBM could deal with the matter. The chair tries hard to persuade the head to relinquish responsibility but she wants to cling on to it, despite her protestations that it takes her away from her main responsibilities.

Fortunately, other people support the chair's argument and the thing that seems to clinch the argument is the SBM reminding everyone that the task is within her job description. The head tries one last throw of the dice ("Er ... excuse me. I mean, I appreciate you taking the load off me but I'm Karen's line manager, so it should be me that decides what she does.") but the chair politely and skilfully defuses this interjection and seeks the views of other governors. This leads to a positive way forward with which everyone, including the head, seems happy.

Handled less effectively, this could have escalated into a difficult situation, with the head digging in her heels and possibly becoming overly emotional, thereby preventing a solution emerging through consensus.

What could the chair do next?

The situation will need careful monitoring. It may turn out that the head isn't able to allow the SBM sufficient freedom to get on with resolving the issue unless the chair continues to insist on the agreement reached at the meeting.

The committee will need to keep the matter under review at the next few meetings.

Your thoughts, observations and ideas

Defining "Challenge"

"Challenge" can mean different things to different people at different times in different situations. There is no universally accepted definition of the word in an educational context and, of course, it has a number of meanings defined in any dictionary.

Perhaps a thesaurus could give a quicker round-up of possible meanings of the verb:

Accost, arouse, beard, brave, call out, claim, confront, dare, defy, demand, dispute, impugn, investigate, object to, provoke, question, require, stimulate, summon, tax, test, throw down the gauntlet, try.

There is an element of aggression implied in many of these synonyms, and that is one of the reasons why governors sometimes feel wary of challenging their headteacher and senior staff, not least because of the response it is likely to provoke.

Nevertheless, it is a good word, especially when balanced with the word "support". Much depends on the motivation and intention that lies behind the challenge. If governors are there to protect and promote the best interests of the children and young people, even over the interests of the staff, then this will mean challenging staff assumptions, behaviour and attitudes from time to time. Simultaneously, it must be recognised that good headteachers challenge themselves continually and welcome challenge from other people, including governors.

This is borne out by references to challenge in the *Governance Handbook*:

Governors should establish "clear processes for overseeing and monitoring school improvement and providing constructive challenge to executive leaders"

"Executive leaders should welcome and enable appropriately robust challenge by providing any data the board requests and responding positively to searching questions."

"These criteria *[relating to the quality of governance]* include a strong focus on how boards use data to challenge and hold the headteacher to account, and how they evaluate their own impact and develop their own skills, and will help ensure that good governance gets the praise it deserves."

We should note the qualifying words "constructive" and "appropriately robust".

The *Competency Framework* offers this definition: "Providing appropriate challenge to the status quo, not taking information or data at face value and always driving for improvement" and adds: "Holding leaders to account is about establishing clear expectations, ensuring clear lines of responsibility, putting in place systems for monitoring appropriately, ensuring evaluation and taking action in response to that evaluation."

Ofsted, likewise, insists on governors' challenge in the inspection handbook:

"Inspectors will consider whether governors ... provide a balance of challenge and support to leaders, understanding the strengths and areas needing improvement at the school."

"Outstanding: Governors systematically challenge senior leaders so that the effective deployment of staff and resources, including the pupil premium, the primary PE and sport premium, Year 7 literacy and numeracy catch-up premium and special educational needs funding, secures excellent outcomes for pupils.

Governors do not shy away from challenging leaders about variations in outcomes for pupil groups and between disadvantaged and other pupils nationally."

Again, the adverb – in this case "systematically" – is important.

So our challenge should be systematic, constructive and appropriately robust, and we should not shy away from doing it.

One of the best and most helpful guides to effective challenge is Ofsted's 2011 report *School Governance: Learning from the best*. Not only is it very clear about the theory, it provides real examples from the schools the authors visited. This extract provides a flavour:

"Providing challenge: All of the outstanding governing bodies visited struck the right balance between supporting leaders and providing constructive challenge, which holds school leaders to account for the quality of the school's provision and its impact on outcomes for pupils. There were three key elements to getting the balance right:

• understanding their role and how it complements but differs from

that of the headteacher
- using the knowledge and experience they bring to enhance leadership
- asking pertinent questions based on the information and knowledge they have about the school.

A high level of challenge was particularly evident at committee level in the schools visited. Governors served on committees where their knowledge and expertise could be used to best effect. Their expertise, understanding of the school's context, and the school performance information that they received enabled them to ask pertinent and insightful questions. Governors skilfully used information from different sources to shape their questions and test out the accuracy of their understanding of the school's performance ... The ultimate question governors came back to was, 'What difference is this going to make for the pupils and how will we know?'

There was evidence that governors in the schools visited also challenged each other. For example, if discussions strayed into operational matters then governors, often the chair of governors, chairs of committees or Trust governors, stepped in to steer the conversation back to a strategic focus."

In an annex, the report offers details of the governing bodies, their context and some of the approaches taken, providing practical examples of how challenge can be offered effectively in different kinds of schools and situations.

Asking the right questions

In practice, challenge nearly always means asking questions – and following up the answers with more questions to get at the heart of the matter.

Because governors are collectively responsible for the effective oversight of virtually all aspects of the school, the areas in which we may need to offer challenge through asking questions are listed in the *Governance Handbook*:

- procedures
- charity and company law duties
- equality
- education (including the curriculum, subjects and topics like RE and sex education, SEND, assessment)

- staffing and performance management
- finance
- safeguarding and pupil welfare
- pupil wellbeing (including behaviour and discipline, exclusions, attendance)
- admissions
- school premises and control and community use of school premises
- conversion to academy status
- school organisational changes
- information sharing
- complaints
- whistleblowing.

The *Governance Handbook* refers several times to "asking the right questions" and provides a number of useful question banks.

- "[Governors] play a vital role in ensuring the best possible education that takes every child as far as their talents allow. Crucially, that means creating robust accountability for executive leaders by using and being familiar with objective data on the performance of pupils, teachers and finances to ask the right questions."
- "Effective boards hold their executive leaders to account for improving pupil and staff performance by asking the right questions. It is essential that boards use, and are familiar with, specific data about their school(s) to help inform these questions."
- "Boards need to make sure that at least once a year they see objective national data so that they are empowered to ask pertinent and searching questions."
- Asking the right questions is equally important in relation to money as it is to educational performance."
- "In summary, everyone on the board needs a strong commitment to the role and to improving outcomes for children; the inquisitiveness to question and analyse; and the willingness to learn."

The message is clear: our pertinent and searching questioning should be based on the analysis of evidence and data. In reality, though, it is seldom an easy task.

Vignette 2

PARENT ENGAGEMENT

PG1: Well, that's not what's being said on Facebook!

Chair: What are they saying, then?

PG1: The new teacher, Mrs Longstreet – they really don't like her. I mean, I'm not saying I agree with that but it is what some parents are saying.

Chair: Can you intervene to stop it?

PG1: Not really. It's free speech, isn't it? I can't control Facebook.

Chair: You can if it's libellous.

Head: This is a growing problem in many schools, not just ours. Social media are great for all sorts of things. As you know, we use text messaging to tell parents of urgent news and so on. The school's official Facebook site is great – but we set the parameters for that, so it guards against a parent having a pop at a teacher. And we have our policy on social media and online bullying. But a very small minority of parents – and some pupils, sadly – abuse social media by seeking out their teachers' Facebook pages and posting some nasty, personal messages.

Chair: That's right. We had a big push on this last year. Maybe we need another campaign to raise awareness ...

FG: Oh, no! Not another campaign!

Vice chair: I think perhaps we should take a couple of steps backward and consider this more coolly. It's obviously an emotional issue, but there are several aspects to it we need to think through.

PG2: Such as?

VC: Well, there's obviously the issue about the policies on social media but there's also a question about Mrs Longstreet's capability ...

Chair: Er, hold on. If we're going to start discussing individual teachers' performance, we should make this a confidential item. But we're not in possession of all the facts anyway, are we? So we really shouldn't talk about it here. I agree that the matter is urgent – well, the harassment of teachers by parents using Facebook and so on ...

Head: If I may? I agree that we need to defuse the matter and separate out the different strands we need to address. I don't intend discussing Mrs Longstreet's performance in this or any other meeting, nor would I if it were any other member of staff. I monitor teacher performance through the year, not just through appraisal but also through other more informal approaches.

Chair: And you give us that annual summary of teachers' performance management, which is really helpful.

PG1: That's all well and good but we have a group of parents saying all sorts of nasty things about the teachers. What are we going to do about that? It's urgent. We can't afford to wait for another annual report.

SG: Do we know which parents are posting messages and what they're saying?

PG2: I have a pretty good idea but they don't use their real names so we can't be certain. It's obvious what they're writing, though – and it's not very complimentary.

SG: Presumably it's just parents of children in Year 6?

PG2: Probably.

SG: So we could just focus on all those parents and get a general message out to them about not abusing Facebook.

Head: I'm happy to do that. I could call a meeting …

PG1: But the troublemakers won't come to that, will they, so you'll be punishing the wrong ones.

Head: No, probably not. A letter, perhaps? Or maybe a series of text messages reminding people of the policy? I'll need to think about this.

FG: Can I return to the issue of teacher performance, please? I take the head's point about anonymity and annual reports and so on, but we're supposed to know what the quality of teaching is, aren't we? If Ofsted turned up tomorrow, they could well ask us what we know about it.

SG: Fair point. We have the Pupil Tracker data, of course. That gives us a clear idea of how we're doing. And as far as I recall, the last time we looked at it, we were pretty happy about progress in Year 6.

VC: Well, we weren't altogether happy about the Pupil Premium children's progress. Has that improved since we last looked?

Head: It has, as you'll see at next week's meeting. It's still not where we'd like it to be but we have put a number of new strategies in place that seem to be working. But, as I understand it, that's not what the parents are complaining about on Facebook. Their comments are much more personal.

FG: So how is Mrs Longstreet? We owe her a duty of care.

Head: She's upset, of course but we've talked it through and she's feeling a bit happier now. She's closed down her Facebook page and is avoiding other forms of social media for the time being.

VC: So, we should do something to try to get parents to engage more positively with the school. Maybe this is borne of frustration. I think we do pretty well in trying to involve the parents but there's always that hard-to-reach group and there's always more that could be done, if we had the time and the resources.

Head: I have been giving that a lot of thought. I was talking to a fellow head recently who's recently appointed a Family Liaison worker, part time, and that is having some positive effects. I wondered whether we could look at employing her, too, for maybe a day a week?

Chair: We'll need to run that past the Finance committee but they meet the week after next so we have time to get it on the agenda. My gut feeling is that if we can afford it, we should do it.

PG1: It's been a while since we did a parent survey, hasn't it? If we did one soon and quickly, we could get a better idea of how dissatisfied the parents are – and if they are, at all. If it shows that there's only a small minority of complainers we can use it to put things in their proper perspective.

PG2: Yes, but what if it doesn't?

Head: Then we come clean and acknowledge that we're not doing as well as we should and what we plan to do to improve.

Chair: That gets my vote. How soon could we get the survey out?

Head: Well, if we just target Year 6 parents and use the forthcoming parents' evening to get them to complete it – and offer it online, too, it could be done within a fortnight. Let's keep it short – just two or three questions.

PG1: That sounds good to me. I'll spread the word that that's what we're doing.

Chair: Thanks. So, we may not have cracked it completely but we have a couple of ways forward. Let's keep it under close review and see if things improve.

COMMENTARY

In this vignette we see the governors asking a lot of challenging questions. There are several strands to this issue, which is often the case. The governors, between them, raise questions about parental abuse of staff via social media, teacher performance, pupil progress, parental engagement and parental surveys.

Challenges are offered by governors to the head's management of all these issues, so it gets a little messy and the discussion risks getting out of control and losing focus.

It would be easy for the discussion to descend into an emotional conversation about the named teacher and possibly named parents, which would be inappropriate and unhelpful. The danger of discussing individual teachers' performance is avoided by timely interventions from the chair and head.

The staff governor points out that teacher performance can be seen through pupil tracking data which is shared with the governors. The vice chair questions the rate of progress of Pupil Premium children and the head acknowledges that "it's still not where we'd like it to be" which suggests that there might be something of substance behind the parents' concerns, even if their reactions are out of proportion and targeted unfairly in an abusive manner.

The foundation governor reminds governors of their duty of care and the head says that some actions have been taken to support the teacher – though not by the governors.

The vice chair looks for improved parental engagement and it's clear that the head has already given this some thought. A parental survey is proposed to gauge the full extent of any concerns.

The chair acknowledges that "We may not have cracked it completely" but there is an intention to keep things under review. The big question remains: is this enough? Will the initial problem be solved? What precisely is the problem or problems?

There is a danger that if only a partial solution has been found, ("I'll need to think about this," says the head), the original problem may continue to grow and worsen, involving more dissatisfied parents.

The governors could and perhaps should have focused longer on each of the issues they identified, prioritising them in terms of urgency and importance, then seeking more specific actions to address them.

What could the chair and governors do next?

The chair will need to meet with the head very regularly to monitor the Facebook comments and press for more action if it does not calm down quickly. Governors will need to monitor progress on the issues at the next committee and full governing body meetings. This must include focusing on the progress of the Pupil Premium children, especially. There needs to be a longer debate about the merits of employing a family liaison worker, both in terms of the affordability of the proposal and its likelihood to bring about sufficient improvements. The parental survey should provide the governors with useful information, so they need to ensure they can meet to discuss the outcomes in the near future. If it looks as though there is more parental dissatisfaction than they anticipated, further actions will need to be proposed and implemented.

Your thoughts, observations and ideas

The Human Dimension

The human dimension is rarely considered by the DfE in their advice and guidance to governors. The *Governance Handbook*, in its revised version of January 2017, and accompanying *Competency Framework* stress the need for governors to be skilled and to organise themselves effectively, ensuring they fulfil their statutory duties and self-evaluate in order to improve – all of which are perfectly reasonable. Their expectations are high, quite rightly.

As noted above, Ofsted has published helpful analyses of the characteristics of outstanding governance (and governance in challenging situations). These reports offer more in the way of practical advice and guidance, based on what some governing bodies have achieved.

Every governing board is unique, each being a singular combination of unpaid volunteers from different backgrounds, with different skills, experience and attitudes, varying amounts of time to offer and levels of commitment. Most are not education experts. Some governors may have a background in education, such as ex-headteachers, but their knowledge and experience of the contemporary educational world may be out-of-date. They are often very effective governors but their education background can sometimes prove to be a weakness. Occasionally such governors might side with the head and staff (and vice versa) because they are subconsciously still mainly headteachers rather than governors. We are all biased, whether consciously or unconsciously. To return to a quotation at the very start of the book: "There are three sides to every story: yours ... mine ... and the truth. No one is lying." A wise governor knows this and takes account of it when making judgements.

Those on the governing body may not know each other very well. They may not even like each other. Some may have been governing for a long time, others may be completely new. Chairing may be weak or strong. The clerk might be a formidable professional or someone doing the job at a basic level out of the goodness of their heart, for a pittance. Some governors can be a positive menace, showing all the worst aspects of humanity, bringing governance and governors into disrepute. Most are not like that, fortunately.

School leadership teams, in contrast, are made up of experienced professionals, paid to do a high powered and demanding job. They have been selected for the role and are subject to regular appraisal. Like most professionals, they are fluent in the jargon and acronyms of their profession. In most cases, they know what they are doing and are good at their job, working long hours with a high degree of commitment. They welcome and encourage legitimate challenge. But not all, as is the case in many professions. Some headteachers are burning out. Some are vulnerable, aware of shortcomings they cannot admit. They have to be seen to be in charge even when they feel anything but that. Some, it must be said, lie and deceive. Occasionally, some are sacked. Very rarely, some end up in prison.

In every school the relationship between the governors and the leadership team must be grown over time. The boundaries of their respective roles need to be understood and respected. Mutual expectations need to be realistic. But all the advice, training and guidance in the world won't make the slightest difference if the relationship between the governors and the school leadership team is dysfunctional. Relationships are never perfect, and even when they approach it, they may not stay that way for long.

In the unsnappily titled *What Governing Boards Should Expect from School Leaders and What School Leaders Should Expect from Governing Boards* (NGA, NAHT and ASCL) the respective roles are set out clearly. Governing boards must have:

- the right people round the table
- an understanding of their role and responsibilities
- a good chair
- professional clerking
- good relationships based on trust
- a knowledge of the school – the data, the staff, the children, the parents, and the community
- a commitment to asking challenging questions
- the confidence to have courageous conversations in the interests of the children and young people.

School leaders in return must have:

- an understanding of governance, including acknowledging the role of the school's accountable body
- a willingness to provide information in the most appropriate way in order that the governing board can carry out its role
- a willingness to be challenged
- reasonable time to devote to ensuring professional relationships are

established with governors and trustees
- the skills and understanding to develop effective working relationships with the governing board.

In many schools, these mutual expectations are well established and ensure that both parties work together in harmony. However, in a smaller number of schools, there are many ways in which the relationship can become an obstacle to constructive challenge, with issues on both sides of the relationship.

On the governors' side there might be:

- a desire to challenge but not managing it effectively
- a reluctance to challenge "the experts" for fear of looking foolish or inadequate
- poor team spirit and cohesion in the board, with no solid consensus as to the issues to be challenged
- a lack of training and experience in governance and education
- poor understanding of the purpose of governance
- an overly aggressive approach which fails to take account of the many pressures on the leadership team
- poor understanding of the data
- personal rather than professional agendas, overt or covert
- a reliance on the headteacher for information and a too-trusting attitude
- limited understanding of lines of accountability.

On the school leadership team side we might encounter some of all of the following:

- a desire to be challenged but not managing it effectively
- a lack of understanding of the governors' roles and responsibilities
- a dismissive attitude towards governors as ill-informed do-gooders
- a lack of acceptance of the governors' duty to challenge
- personal dislike of one or more governors
- a lack of patience and tolerance towards non-educational experts
- a lack of trust in the governors' respect for confidentiality
- withholding of evidence showing problems and weaknesses
- misuse of supposed restrictions (e.g. parent governors being denied certain information because are not trusted to maintain confidentiality; staff governors being forbidden to participate in HR issues).

Lack of mutual trust can often be at the heart of the problem. Where this is the case, governors and leaders must face facts and invest time and effort in rebuilding the relationship, perhaps with neutral, external facilitation.

Each school has its own culture and ethos, developed over years. Oddly, it is both hard to pin down yet very obvious, usually from the minute one enters the school. It may have been grown deliberately and for positive reasons – the culture of high expectations of everyone in the school, including governors – or it may have developed haphazardly and be less than healthy. How do teachers behave, for example, when the staffroom door closes? What do they say about the children and the families they come from? Does one group or an individual wield oppressive power and influence? I have experienced schools where the teaching assistants, collectively, seemed to dominate the staff and the headteacher. Very unusual, it must be said, but I've come across another where no one dared criticise the caretaker, who was all-powerful.

How well do the governors know the staff and vice versa? Even in a small school this can be hard to achieve and be well-nigh impossible in a large one. If governors are meant to be strategic ("eyes up, hands off"), should they invest time in getting to know the staff anyway? Do the staff really understand the governors' role? More often than not, they don't. Understanding governance is not part of teacher training and unless a member of staff is also a governor, they may never come in contact with governors. Yet ultimately governors are responsible for staffing matters and have a duty of care towards the school's employees so both sides have an intrinsic stake in knowing and understanding each other.

Most importantly, how well *do* the governors and headteacher (and leadership team) know and understand one another? What are their attitudes to one another?

At the heart of it all lies the relationship between the headteacher and the chair of governors. In a healthy relationship, these two will meet regularly and be able to talk to each other frankly and in confidence when necessary, sharing thoughts, feelings and ideas in a safe space where mutual challenge is the norm. However, this can become a little too cosy and exclusive, and it's hard to guard against it. Where the head and chair are in cahoots, the school is heading for trouble.

Sometimes heads find that the chair is never available when they need them or, on the contrary, is in school far too often, getting under their feet. Both situations are dysfunctional and it's hard to say which is worse.

If challenge is to be regular and effective, the relationship between the head and SLT on the one side and chair and governors on the other must be disinterestedly professional, each group respecting the other.

Vignette 3

JOINING A MAT

Chair: Which brings us to the main item for this meeting – the MAT. Has everyone seen the paper on our online platform?

(General agreement)

Head: As I think all governors know, we have a number of options before us. We can't stay as we are, as a standalone academy ... well, I mean, we can for a while but we'll face increasing pressure from the RSC to either set up a new MAT or join one of the two existing ones in the area, so it's probably better to decide our own fate than have one forced on us.

PG1: I understand what you're saying but I remember when we chose to become an academy it was sold to us as being about having more autonomy, wasn't it? If we join a MAT, we won't be free to do what we want, will we? It'll depend on what the MAT wants. At the very least, we'll have to make some compromises.

PG2: I agree. We had long discussions about leaving the LA and we agreed to do it because we'd be able to choose where we bought our services from and save money. And, to be fair, that's what we've done. Won't a MAT tell us where to get our services from?

Chair: This is covered in the paper – it's in the fourth paragraph, I think. The point is, if we set up our own MAT, we can set the tone for all the other schools that join us, so we're in the driving seat. If we join an existing MAT, we'd have to negotiate more – but we could still have more control than we did with the LA.

Head: It's a trade-off, for sure. We need to think three or five years ahead to try to imagine what the educational landscape will look like before we make any hard decisions now. That's why I included the paragraphs about our vision and values at the start of the paper.

CG1: I get that but we haven't got time this evening for a lot of navel-gazing. Can we cut to the chase? What do you think we should do?

Head: My own preference would be for us to set up as a MAT, then recruit other schools over the next few years. There's a danger in growing too fast, of course, so I think we should try to pace ourselves carefully.

CG: Will the RSC allow us to do that? Aren't they cracking the whip?

Head: There's pressure, certainly, but it's not oppressive. We have room for manoeuvre.

SG: The staff think it's best if we make the running, by setting up our own MAT, while we've got time.

PG1: But have we got the time and resources to do that? Won't it be a distraction? I mean, we're outstanding now but we haven't been inspected for seven years. If Ofsted turn up and downgrade us, we'd have to focus on that, not setting up some new organisation.

PG2: No one's said anything yet about the two MATs we could join. I've read the discussion paper and they both look like good options to me, though I know which one I prefer. It seems to me it would be a lot easier to join something that exists, rather than setting something up from scratch.

Chair: We're dodging about a bit from one aspect to another, aren't we? My fault! Can I bring us back to first principles? The head's right to stress vision and values and we don't need to go over those in detail, but they do suggest the way forward – or at least set the parameters for this discussion. I mean, we wouldn't want to join a MAT that didn't share our basic values, would we, and I think that rules out the Fountain Trust.

CG2: Why?

Chair: Well, if you look at their track record, they are big and plan to get a lot bigger. They are paying their CEO a small fortune already and I've heard rumours that they're planning to get rid of all the local governing bodies in their academies. Whereas we value the family atmosphere of our school and I hope we all value our role as a governing body. We wouldn't want to sacrifice those things, would we?

SG: Definitely not. The staff are not keen on Fountain.

PG2: But isn't there something to be said for joining a big, strong MAT? Isn't it likely to provide real security when budgets are getting tighter?

PG1: I'm with the chair on this one. I don't like the sound of Fountain.

Head: If we could return to the discussion paper? I have set out the options, including the pros and cons of each, as I see them. Shall I just run through them briefly, then we can discuss each one in turn?

Chair: Yes, that makes sense.

CG2: Agreed.

Head: OK. So, option 1 is joining Fountain Academy Trust. They are big and getting bigger, as you've said, but are very popular and, generally speaking, standards have improved in most of the schools that have joined. They want us in their MAT – in fact, they're very keen. Option 2 is Green Valley Trust. They're much smaller but are planning to grow slowly. I think their values are closer to ours but the schools aren't doing as well as the ones in Fountain. They are reasonably keen for us to join but I sense that they may feel a bit threatened by us. Then there's the possibility of us setting up our own MAT. Yes, it will take quite a lot of preparation, but no more than when we first set up as an academy. The beauty of it is that we can set the terms and standards for anyone else joining.

PG1: But what if no other school wants to join?

Head: Well, we have put out feelers to local schools and at least three would be keen to join us, so I don't think it would be a problem.

Chair: Thanks for that clear summary. I want to remind everyone that we're not here to make a decision tonight. This is just the first stage in the decision-making process. It's important that we all re-read the discussion paper and then ask all the questions we need to before we jump in any particular direction.

Head: And I want to stress that I don't have all the answers yet but please keep feeding me your thoughts and questions – they all help to clarify the choices we have to make. This is obviously a really important decision and it will affect what happens for years to come, so I'm not rushing.

CG1: OK, but how long have we got, realistically?

Chair: Well, probably till the end of next term. I mean, that sounds like ages away but we all know how quickly it will come around, so it really matters that we all continue to think about the options. So, unless anyone has anything else to say about it right now, I suggest we move on.

COMMENTARY

This vignette shows a head and chair working together effectively and not colluding with one another in raising a potentially very charged issue.

The discussions are at an early stage. The chair and head seem to have worked together on the discussion paper which has been made available for all governors to read. It's not clear that everyone has actually read it and, more importantly, fully understood it.

Some of the governors remember the process when the school became a standalone academy. The chair and head are open about the issues that deserve discussion and seem to encourage all governors to contribute, even though this means the discussion gets slightly blown off course ("We're dodging about a bit from one aspect to another, aren't we?"). The chair tries to refocus the discussion on vision and values in order to consider what the academy might gain and lose from joining a MAT. Various governors start to offer their preferences, though it's too early for that to be managed properly at this stage. The head's intervention is crucial, bringing everyone back to pros and cons set out in the paper. The options are clear and the governors have had an opportunity at this early stage to ask questions and raise issues for further consideration. There is a range of opinion and the head and chair are now in a better position to understand that range and think through how best to respond. They remind the governors that they are only at an early stage, that the paper needs to be reread, questions asked and addressed, and the decision not rushed.

The chair and head have managed this initial discussion effectively. Along the way, governors have raised challenges about a possible loss of autonomy, especially in relation to purchasing services; the role and influence of the RSC; and the danger of getting distracted from the main task of raising standards.

There was a danger in this scenario of the head and chair working too closely together and preventing proper discussion, especially if they favoured a particular outcome. Although the head does express a preference, others are encouraged to express theirs and there doesn't appear to be a stitch-up.

What could the chair and head do next?
They set out the next steps at the end of the discussion but, if they haven't done so already, will need to plan a sequence of meetings to enable the next stages to be worked through systematically. They might need a post-mortem following this meeting to confirm their joint understanding of the various positions taken by different governors and to consider how best to take account of the different views expressed.

Your thoughts, observations and ideas

Vignette 4

SAFEGUARDING

Pupil welfare committee meeting
Head: So, now you've had a chance to read my safeguarding report, does anyone have any questions?
Chair: Anyone? Anything?
(Silence)
Well, I'd like to thank the headteacher on behalf of the committee for another excellent report. I'm sure we all feel we can relax, knowing that everything's under control. So, next item. E .... oh, yes, parental complaints. Bryony?
Head: Sorry, madam chair, but I'm not sure we should move on quite so rapidly. I mean, there is an awful lot of detail in the report and I'm surprised that no one has any questions. There are quite a few policy changes in there, and I've

been frank about some of the areas where we've fallen down. For example, I questioned the role of the safeguarding governor in the report. I know Femi isn't here right now but I would have expected some feedback on my proposals. It's in the report. Page 17, I think you'll find … there it is, para 21, bullet point 18 …

FG: I'm sorry, I haven't brought my copy, so …

Clerk: It is on the governors' intranet, like all the other papers for the meeting.

FG: I'm sorry, as I've said before, I don't really do intranets and suchlike. I'm rather old-fashioned, I know, but has anyone got a paper copy I could share?

PG: Here, I printed it off. You can borrow mine. I've got my tablet with me. Mind, if I'd realised just how long it is, I wouldn't have bothered.

Chair: Very well. So, if we can all look at the offending article …

Head: Yes, well … in a nutshell, I'm suggesting that we scrap the role because, quite frankly, it's not fit for purpose.

Chair: What do you mean? Are you saying Femi's not up to it? That's hardly fair, and he's not here to defend himself.

Head: No, that's not what I'm saying, if you'll take the trouble to read what I've written. It's got nothing to do with whoever fulfils the role. It's the point of the role itself. I just don't think it's working in practice. It seemed like a good idea three years ago and I know quite a few governing bodies have done something similar, but for it to be truly effective, the governor would have to be very proactive and give more time to it than Femi can. And I don't think any governors here have the time to take it on. Besides which, if I can be frank, I think it lets everyone else off the hook, which is wrong. Ofsted see safeguarding as a golden thread that runs through every aspect of the school and its work, so leaving it to just one governor is dangerous.

PG: I think the head has a point. We are here to discuss her report, aren't we?

Chair: And that is what we're doing. So let's focus on this issue; should we abolish the role of safeguarding governor?

FG: I'm not sure I can express a valid view at this stage, as I haven't read the report yet.

PG: Well, we can't really defer this decision till next time, can we? Our agenda for the next meeting is already full, as I understand it.

Clerk: Yes, that's true.

Chair: It's not a particularly complicated issue. I don't think your not having read the report should prevent us reaching a decision.

FG: Well, I'm not really comfortable with that …

PG: Oh, come on! Let's just make a decision and move on, otherwise we'll be here all night.

Chair: So – all those in favour of getting rid of the safeguarding governor? *(Notes the number of hands raised)*

> Those against?
> *(Notes the number of hands raised)*
> Motion carried. Now, Bryony, parental complaints ...

COMMENTARY

The initial reaction to the chair's invitation to governors to ask any questions of the headteacher's report – deadly silence – suggests either a complacent or lazy board of governors.

As we see later in the vignette, the report is a long one ("As I say it's in the report. Page 17, I think you'll find ... there it is, para 21, bullet point 18.") so perhaps some governors might be forgiven for not having absorbed every last detail of it – and perhaps such a long and detailed report could be summarised for governors – but it seems likely that none of the governors has actually read it and at least one hasn't got access to it in the meeting.

A governing board that doesn't prepare properly for meetings is ineffective and incapable of offering proper challenge. If the papers are not available seven days before the meeting then there could be a problem with the clerking, but if the clerk isn't getting all the paperwork on time, others may also be to blame. In this instance, it looks as though the clerk and headteacher are efficient and governors have access to an intranet which holds all the necessary and relevant documents for the meeting – but they don't all make use of it.

In the vignette it falls to the headteacher to try to provoke some discussion and debate. This should not be necessary if they are well-informed and actively engaged.

The chair's language is patronising ("if we can all look at the offending article ...") and she reacts too defensively to the headteachers' proposals to remove the role of the safeguarding governor. These attitudes mean that the head has an uphill struggle in persuading the governors to consider her proposals in any depth. She has to challenge them, rather than vice versa.

A decision is made, based on a vote, but it seems to be very uninformed and the rest of the head's report is left unconsidered, due to the pressures of time.

What could the headteacher and the other governors do to address this failure to challenge?

The relationship between the head and the chair matters a lot in this instance. One might feel that the head has probably tried to work with the chair but hasn't managed to convince her of the governors' duty to challenge and the chair doesn't want to or is incapable of providing the leadership the board needs. It is very hard for a headteacher in these circumstances to make any headway since the chair is such an obstacle. If there are governors who are frustrated with the chair's approach, the head could perhaps seek to gain their trust and gently push for a change of chair at the next opportunity, though this could backfire easily.

It really is up to the governors, collectively, to assert their power in recognising the weakness of the chair and either pressing for rapid improvement in the chair's performance or finding a new one. This will demand that at least one governor is prepared to stand for election and for sufficient governors to back him or her.

While this may seem radical, if they don't bite the bullet, they will be vulnerable in any Ofsted inspection.

This is a faith school, since it has at least one foundation governor. It may be that the diocese could intervene and persuade the chair to stand down – but before that one or more governors would need to blow the whistle and alert the diocese to the problem.

Your thoughts, observations and ideas

How to Offer Effective Challenge

Imagine, for a few minutes, that you are an Ofsted inspector. You are informed that you are due to inspect Bash Street Junior School within a few weeks. You know nothing about the school, so what do you do?

Inevitably, you have to look at any and all published information about the school. This will include Analyse School Performance service and the associated Inspection Dashboard. You will look at the school's website. You will ask the school to send you a variety of documents, but only at the last minute.

On the basis of what you have read, you will need to formulate a hypothesis about the school and the grade you are likely to award it.

During the inspection, lasting a maximum of two days, though just one if the school's last rating was Good, the main task is to test your hypothesis against the reality of what you experience, discuss and observe.

At the end of the inspection day you have to tell school leaders what you think about the school and what grades you are minded to award.

You then have a few days to write your report, in which any statement you make must be supported by evidence and which will be quality assured by at least one other person. The report will normally be in the public domain within three weeks.

This is a testing and demanding schedule.

Now consider the perspective of a school governor. The chances are you are familiar with your school, depending on how long you have served and whether you have one or more children in the school.

You have access not just to all the historical data about your school but a lot of current information, too. You may know the headteacher and at least some other staff reasonably well. You may well have visited the school on several occasions for a variety of purposes. You have, perhaps, several more years to serve as a governor and many more opportunities to get to know the school well.

But you're not an Ofsted inspector. You're not an education expert. You depend to a large extent on the professionals providing you with evidence and an explanation of what it all means.

So could you learn anything useful from how inspectors judge schools, allowing for the fact that they may not always get everything right?

I would like to suggest that there is much to be learned, but avoiding any notion that governors should aspire to become *de facto* Ofsted inspectors.

An external perspective

First, inspectors have an objective external perspective. They don't have a personal connection with the school. They see lots of other schools. They have a background in education and are regularly trained and their work overseen by peers.

Governors can't afford to wait for Ofsted to turn up in order to gain this external perspective. If the school was previously graded Outstanding, in theory the inspectors will never return. Good schools receive a short inspection after three years to check whether they are still good – or better, or worse. Only in schools Requiring Improvement or which are Inadequate do governors meet Ofsted inspectors on a regular basis.

While I would not wish on all governors the experience of governing a school in these latter categories, it certainly provides a sharp baptism of fire in how to scrutinise, monitor and evaluate improvement in a short time.

Governors in maintained schools can no longer rely on free advice from a team of local authority school advisers. Where these still exist, their efforts are focused exclusively on the schools causing greatest concern. If your school is Good or Outstanding, you will have to buy in any external review. The same applies to single academies. In a multi-academy trust, there should be the potential of school-to-school review. In the larger MATs there may well be a dedicated school improvement service that local governing bodies can access.

Where governors have real concerns about the quality of their school, investing in a professional school review may be a necessary and valuable way forward.

Data and other quantitative information

Second, inspectors interrogate a variety of sets of data about the school, all of which are also available to governors. The range and variety of the data can be bewildering and daunting to governors unused to statistical analysis. This is acknowledged in the *Governance Handbook*, which offers this guidance:

> "It is essential that every board has at least one person with the skills to understand and interpret the full detail of the educational performance and the financial data available. These individuals should make sure that the board has a correct understanding of the school's perfor-

mance and finances as presented and explained by executive leaders. They should identify from the data the issues that need to be discussed and addressed as a priority. Others on the board should learn from them and undertake training where this is needed to improve their confidence and skills in looking at and discussing issues arising from data.

While boards may decide to establish a committee to look in detail at performance data, everyone on the board should be able to engage fully with discussions about data in relation to the educational and financial performance of their school. If they cannot, they should undertake appropriate training or development to enable them to do so. This includes MAT boards who should not leave this function solely to LGBs, where they are in place, but should themselves be familiar with and interrogate key performance data, while avoiding duplication of roles and functions."

Much of the data is, inevitably, historical. Analyse School Performance reports, for example, are published up to a year after the tests taken by pupils in order to allow for resits and validation. The main data sources are given overleaf.

While this book is not about explaining how to interpret and use these various data sets, it is vital that governors are aware of what they are and how they can use them to challenge school leaders. They can find this out by accessing training and information, which are reasonably widely available through local authorities, the NGA and private providers.

Document	Source	What it includes	When published
Ofsted report	Ofsted	• overall effectiveness • effectiveness of leadership and management • quality of teaching, learning and assessment • personal development, behaviour and welfare • outcomes for pupils	Usually three weeks after inspection
Compare School Performance tables	DfE via www.gov.uk	• performance of different groups in most recent national tests • absence and pupil population data • workforce data • financial data	Updated annually; online resource
Analyse School Performance service and Inspection Dashboard	DfE and Ofsted	• attainment and pupil progress compared to the national and local averages • performance by different groups of pupils • patterns of performance	Updated annually; online resource
FFT Aspire: Fischer Family Trust dashboard	Fischer Family Trust	• attainment and pupil progress compared to the national average • performance in different subjects • any under-performing groups of pupils • school context and its effect on performance • pupil attendance compared to the national average	Updated regularly; online resource
EEF Families of Schools database	Education Endowment Foundation	• interactive tool that allows schools to compare the performance of their pupils to other schools with similar characteristics • helps facilitate collaboration between schools facing similar challenges so they may learn from one another	Updated regularly; online resource
Schools financial benchmarking	DfE via www.gov.uk	• enables maintained schools to compare their spending in detail with other maintained schools, consider their comparative performance and think about how to improve their efficiency • academies can view comparable statistical data for income and expenditure in academies nationally	Updated regularly; online resource

The main sources of data on current performance are:

Document	Source	What it includes	When published
Pupil tracking data	Many different ones available to schools, e.g Classroom Monitor, School Pupil Tracker Online, schools' own	• varies according to the product • collates and interprets pupil performance data across the school and curriculum • should be anonymised for governors	Continuous
Headteacher reports to the governing board	No standard model or format; often follows the headings of an Ofsted report	• varies from one head to another • *Governance Handbook* suggests: – pupil learning and progress – pupil applications, admissions, attendance and exclusions – staff absence, recruitment, retention, morale and performance – the quality of teaching	Three or more times per year
School self-evaluation (SEF)	No standard model or format; often follows the headings of an Ofsted report	varies from one school to another	Usually annually but should be updated regularly through the year

Qualitative information and evidence

In addition to the hard data, inspectors and governors should have access to a range of other forms of information, including:

- progress reports on strategic and improvement plans
- feedback from stakeholders
- school visits.

In these areas of softer information, school inspectors may employ a variety of approaches, including:

- triangulation: asking questions of different groups and comparing the answers
- observation of teaching and learning
- work sampling
- analysing stakeholder views of the school
- discussion between inspectors, where possible.

Most importantly, inspectors talk to headteachers throughout the inspection, sharing their judgements, observations and arguments. Heads are encouraged to defend their own judgements with evidence and present further evidence where necessary. It is a serious professional conversation, not a cat-and-mouse game.

Opportunities for challenge: the school improvement cycle

Throughout any single school year there will be some prime opportunities for governors to offer challenge, and the annual school improvement cycle provides governors with a clear schedule.

Assuming that the school has a clearly articulated vision and a strategic plan in place for reaching it, the annual cycle should represent a systematic process for improving vital aspects of the school year-on-year, within that broader context.

Each year the school should update its own self-evaluation by asking questions such as "How well are we doing, compared to last year?", "How well are we doing, compared to other similar schools?" and "What more do we need to achieve this year?"

This latter question, especially, offers a prime opportunity for governors to challenge the school's aspirations of its staff and pupils/students. Most heads are ambitious for their young people and relish a challenge but there are perverse disincentives built into the education system. For example, the head's pay rise will depend on measurable outcomes, including some objectives around improved school performance. It would be saintly for a head not to want to set reasonably easily achieved targets, but some heads are saintly!

Agreeing on targets that are both challenging but not totally unrealistic should put the head and the governors on their mettle. If agreement is reached very quickly, with little debate, it may indicate a lack of real rigour and challenge from the governors.

Action plans for improvement will be enshrined in a school development or improvement plan. Much of the detail of the action plans will be down to the professional expertise and judgement of specialist staff, so governors should step into the background over the writing of the plans, but ensure that systems, processes and dates for monitoring and evaluating are written into them. Subsequently they can and should play a vital role in monitoring and evaluating progress against the targets.

Effective monitoring and evaluation – and challenge – depend largely on asking the right questions based on the information available.

Vignette 5
PUPIL PREMIUM

Chair: So, on to Key Stage 4. Headteacher?

Head: Thank you, chair. We've maintained a significantly stronger position for two years in terms of student achievement at KS4. The Inspection Dashboard confirmed a significant improvement at KS4, to the levels that we should be expecting given our relatively able intake, and we are maintaining that this year. 73% achieved a strong pass in English and maths compared to 64% in 2015 and 76% in 2016.

Chair: That's good to hear. We were quite concerned about the dip in outcomes a couple of years ago, weren't we? So what do you think has made the difference?

Head: We think it's mainly down to better tracking and intervention, which is now embedded in all our KS4 processes. We can see that English and Maths achievement is very strong now. You'll remember the worrying decline in English which we identified previously.

FG: Is the picture equally good for all students, right across the board? I mean, what about Pupil Premium students, for example?

Head: Fair question. It is still something that concerns me – but not as much as it once did. As you know, we don't have that many Pupil Premium students compared to most schools and there is a risk that we don't focus on them enough but I can report that although the gap in attainment for Pupil Premium students is still large – and larger than it should be, it is closing.

FG: Fast enough?

Head: Not as fast as I'd like but at the same time the gap in Pupil Premium progress has narrowed dramatically, and that has to be good news. We are monitoring this group especially closely and the current year 11 are in a strong position to maintain these improvements.

PG: That's reassuring, but do we know why the gap was larger last year?

Head: We have looked at this very closely and there are a number of factors. One that we couldn't really do anything about was that there were several students who did not attend school during Year 11 but remained on the school roll, so they were counted against our overall performance.

PG: What do we know about why they didn't attend? Were they school phobics or something?

Head: Er ... bear with me ... OK, here it is. So, three students were under full-time education by the medical needs service and two were allocated a full-time place at the FE College at the request of the LA. The problem there is that the

College and LA do not have a DfE roll for KS4 so we agreed to the LA request to have them on the school roll. I hope you all agree that that was the right thing to do, as a VA school? We did discuss it in committee at the time, but it was a while ago now.

Chair: I wasn't committee chair then but I was on the committee and I do remember the issue being discussed. We did agree with the policy, as it seemed to be in line with our vision and values.

PG: OK, that seems fair, but it's a shame the DfE counts them when there's no way we could affect their outcomes. Do we know what the picture would look like if we didn't count those five students?

Head: Yes. If we exclude those students from the data, the 5 "good passes" in English and Maths attainment for the PP cohort rises from 53 percent to 57 percent and the gap reduces to 22 percent. Similarly, the English and Maths progress figures rise from 60 percent to 66 percent and from 67 percent to 72 percent respectively.

FG: So it certainly shows that we are doing better for the Pupil Premium students we can have an influence on. But is it enough?

Head: Well, if we look at the Inspection Dashboard again, it shows FSM VA for a "good pass" at national levels for all EBacc subjects apart from English but significantly above in Humanities. So that's reasonably reassuring.

FG: What about the non-EBacc subjects?

Head: There is more work to be done to close the gap in some subjects: the overall VA of the 29 Free School Meal students was significantly below the national average for that group.

Chair: This helps us understand what happened in previous years and gives us something to measure against but of course we need to focus on the Pupil Premium students we have in school now. Have we got any PP students on roll now who are not actually attending school?

Head: No, none in the current cohort.

FG: So, if they don't do as well as they should, it will be the school's fault?

Chair: That's a bit harsh!

Head: No, it's a fair point. I will make sure that you get regular reports about those students in particular – not by name, of course – so you can see what impact we're having.

COMMENTARY

This discussion focuses on some very specific data about the performance of Pupil Premium students. It could be inferred that the fine detail has not been shared with the governors, since the head has to look through it to find the answer to a question ("Er ... bear with me ... OK, here it is.") This is not good practice and puts the governors at a disadvantage. Nobody at the meeting raises it as an issue, though.

Despite this, the parent and foundation governor, especially, ask a series of short, well-focused questions which interrogate the headteacher very effectively. Towards the end, the questions become very sharply worded ("So, if they don't do as well as they should, it will be the school's fault?") but the head accepts the validity of the enquiry ("No, it's a fair point").

Despite the possibility that the detail has not been shared with governors, the head comes across as being frank and open to fair criticism. Are his answers excuses or explanations? Initially, they could be interpreted as excuses but because the head provides detailed answers to the governors' probing questions, it's fair to regard them as factual explanations.

The chair takes something of a back seat in the discussion but intervenes effectively when necessary, for example, by refocusing the discussion on the present: "This helps us understand what happened in previous years and gives us something to measure against but of course we need to focus on the Pupil Premium students we have in school now. Have we got any PP students on roll now who are not actually attending school?"

What could the chair and governors do next?

The chair should talk to the head about the governors not being given the same data as the head possessed to make sure this doesn't happen again. The chair and governors need to make sure the head continues to provide them with regular updates on student progress and performance so that they can be fully confident of the head's assertions and explanations.

Your thoughts, observations and ideas

Making Use of Data and Information: questions, questions, questions

Interrogating data sets, however intelligently, can become but should not be an end in itself. As the *Governance Handbook* advises us, governors should identify from the data the issues that need to be discussed and addressed as a priority.

This entails asking questions, which sounds simple but lies at the heart of the challenge of "challenge".

Questions about questions

Which questions should we ask?

There is no shortage of ready-made questions. There are substantial banks of questions in the *Governance Handbook*, especially in the sections on accountability and financial performance. The Ofsted handbook also lists the many areas of school life that inspectors wish to know about, with substantial lists of criteria and indicators of performance, which can very easily be turned into banks of questions for governors to ask. Separate Ofsted guidance on safeguarding (*Inspecting Safeguarding in Early Years, Education and Skills Settings*) contains a list of descriptors under the heading "The signs of successful safeguarding arrangements" which provide the reader with a ready-made checklist of topics to question.

The problems that governors face are less to do with what to ask as when, how, how many and to whom?

When?

Timing is everything. A full governing board meeting may offer few opportunities for in-depth questioning, simply because of the pressures of time-keeping and a full agenda. That doesn't mean no questions should be asked. Rather, it means that any questions must be sharply focused and relevant, based on an understanding of the detail. Committees offer better opportunities for multiple questions since they have a more limited set of terms of reference, focusing on more specific and interconnected areas of school life. More informal occasions, such as a learning walk, can also offer great opportunities for questions.

How?

The tone of voice we use, the way we phrase our question and our unconscious body language can all have an effect on what kind of a response we get. So much depends upon the nature and quality of the relationship between the governors, individually and collectively, and the head and staff. If there's a tension between the various parties, any slight misjudgement in phrasing a challenging question can result in a defensive and/or emotional response. Investing in the governor-staff relationship can defuse potential difficulties. But even where relationships are based on trust and mutual respect, if we continually ask "robust", "searching" and "probing" questions, as the DfE and Ofsted expect us to do, it can still cause the occasional upset, since heads and teachers, like governors, are human beings.

How many?

Getting to the truth often demands not just one question but many. The follow-up and the follow-up to the follow-up are often necessary. A competent head usually has a ready answer to any question, which is a good thing! That initial answer may, though, be a summary or be superficial. Getting beneath the "professional" answer requires skill and persistence. Once again, though, there is a danger that relentless questioning on a point of detail can alienate the head and other governors, so knowing when to let up is vital. Forensic questioning is what we should aim for: well-honed, specific questions based on a sound understanding of the facts.

To whom?

Inevitably, the headteacher is the person to whom we are likely to ask most questions, but it is dangerous (and tiring for the head) to rely on him or her for all the answers. We should avoid creating unnecessary work for the head and make sure that we have done our research thoroughly. It is good practice for the board to invite a range of staff members to attend their meetings – both full board meetings and committee meetings – from time to time to enable governors to ask what's happening in different subjects and year groups.

How do we know if the answers are reliable and honest?

When interviewing groups of governors during an inspection, inspectors sometimes ask them "How would you know if your head was lying to you?" This is a provocative question, designed to unearth any lack of rigour in the way governors challenge their school leaders, rather than to suggest that heads are liars!

Understandably, heads often wish to present information in the best possible light, so more negative evidence might be glossed over or omitted, consciously or unconsciously. They may inadvertently overload governors with irrelevant data, for fear of being accused of holding something back. They may not fully understand the data (and not realise this) or have misunderstood parts of it. Other school staff may know more than the head about some aspects of the school, though the head may prefer to be the sole conduit of all information to the governors.

Triangulation can be the key to resolving this tricky issue. If the matter in question is essentially quantitative, there will often be several different data sets that can be interrogated and compared in order to identify an accurate answer. If our question is based on a careful analysis of available and accurate data, answers can be checked and double-checked – not, perhaps, immediately, but once the questioner has had time to compare the answer with the data.

When the question is about an aspect of school that is less statistically measurable, such as pupil morale or the school's ethos, it becomes harder for both parties to be certain of the validity of the answer. We can ask ourselves whether our visits to the school and conversations with staff and pupils support the head's view of the school. Even so, hard data can sometimes shed light on qualitative aspects of school performance, such as a record of racist incidents, attendance data or a recent survey of parental opinions.

Telling the difference between a valid explanation and an excuse is not easy but often depends on the fine detail.

Pupil performance: if, for example, the head argues that the reason for a drop in performance is due to a range of external factors, like a change to the National Curriculum and its assessment, that is likely to be an excuse, since the changes will have applied to all similar schools, not all of which may have seen a similar decline. If the explanation is that a key member of staff was absent for several weeks due to a serious illness just prior to SATs week, then that is more likely to be valid – though not necessarily a sufficient explanation.

Quality of teaching: if the head judges most of the teaching in the school to be outstanding but pupil progress in some areas is less good than it should be, we can use pupil performance data to clarify and challenge the accuracy of the head's judgments of teaching quality.

Finance: if the cost of employing supply teachers has increased dramatically compared to previous years, it could be due to unavoidable factors such as a flu epidemic but could also mask a problem of low staff morale or frequent absenteeism by one or more teachers. Simply reading budget reports may not tell us more than the fact that the numbers have gone up. A good budget sheet will have a column for explanations of variances, which is a good starting point, but may still not identify an underlying cause. In this instance we would need to see staff absence data to see if there are any recurring patterns and take into consideration any linked information, such as parental complaints or staff grievances.

What do we do if we find they're not?

If the headteacher denies governors the full picture of the school, warts and all, even Ofsted recognise that it is very hard for governors to do their job, as this quotation from an annual report from the head of Ofsted (*The Report of Her Majesty's Chief Inspector of Education, Children's Services and Skills 2013/14*) shows:

> "from the results of our study of 114 schools that had declined to be less than good ... The governing bodies ... relied heavily on the judgement of the headteacher, and the chair of governors often had too close and 'cosy' a relationship with the headteacher ... we found that governors were entirely unaware of problems or had discovered them too late to secure improvement by the time of the inspection. In some cases, this was because the schools' leaders had not given governors access to the full performance information. In others, it appeared likely ... that governors had been presented with partial or misleading data. *In circumstances like this, it is hard to see how governors can hold schools to account for their performance or fulfil their vital strategic role.*" [emphasis added]

Does this mean that we are powerless in the face of a head who is evasive or fails to understand the nature of legitimate challenge? While the majority of heads welcome and encourage challenge, some do not. Improving the openness of communication between the governors and the headteacher is achievable but may call for courage, sensitivity, intelligence and persistence – and the need for the governing board to remain united around its purpose: getting to the truth. Lest we forget, the head is accountable to the governing board.

Some governors might feel that the head's performance management process might be the right forum to address shortcomings. It might be, depending on when it falls due, but the danger is that it puts off dealing with the immediate problem, and performance management is not intended to be a substitute for any disciplinary procedure.

The chair of governors should have a frank and direct conversation with the head in a one-to-one meeting to address the issues, acting with the full backing of the governing board. The chair must be confident that the governors will support him or her if and when the headteacher reacts negatively. This meeting should provide the head with an opportunity to amend his or her attitude and behaviour. If he or she is willing to change, then the governors will need to monitor the extent to which matters improve – or not.

While this is happening, governors will need to build a case, an audit trail, to show when and how they have been misled or starved of all the facts. Seeking external help is a must, even if it means paying for it, in order to be sure of their ground. If they can prove to their own satisfaction that they have a strong case, then they need to instigate the appropriate Human Resources policies for tackling the problem. This will probably involve activating a capability policy (again, after seeking advice from the relevant professional body, such as a Human Resources team). Working through the stages of the capability procedure may resolve the issue, and often does.

It could, in some circumstances, involve suspension of the headteacher and/or lead to dismissal, though this can take a very long time, during which the school would have to continue paying the head's salary and the salary of a temporary replacement, so it is not to be undertaken lightly. Ultimately, it could lead to an industrial tribunal, where the chair could be cross-examined by experts in what is in effect a trial.

It is not surprising that few governing bodies are prepared to go this far, though some have done.

Vignette 6

PUPIL BEHAVIOUR

Chair: The recent Governors' Day in school seems to have been a great success and we'd like to repeat it next year. Thanks to everyone who took part and to the school for making it so involving and interesting.

Head: Thank you, chair. From the staff's point of view, it went well and they feel they know the governors better as a result. But, since we always want to get better, is there anything from the governors' point of view that we need to improve?

PG: Well, we got round all the classrooms and saw some great teaching but there were one or two cases where the children weren't behaving that well. I mean, the teachers did well with them but they did take up a lot of the teachers' time. I worry about the other children in the class. Are they getting the attention they need?

Chair: Clearly, we're not going to talk about individual children or teachers but is that something you could comment on, please?

Head: Yes, by all means. I think I know which classes and children you're referring to. I'm sure governors will remember the debate we had in the pupil welfare committee about admitting a small number of children that had been excluded from other schools. Clearly, these are children with challenging behaviour, due to their family backgrounds and previous experiences.

CG: Yes, I was at that meeting. We were faced with a bit of an ultimatum by the LA because we had some spaces for additional children so we couldn't really say no. But we did talk about the options and it came down to our vision and values in the end. I mean, we can't really claim to be an inclusive school if we refuse to accept some children.

Head: That's right. But we did insist on a reasonable level of additional support for those children and they all have TA hours attached to them.

Chair: Have any parents raised any concerns?

Head: Initially, yes. One or two parents were understandably concerned about the impact of the children on the class but I spoke to them all individually and went through with them why we were taking on the new children and what support would be put in place, including extra training for the staff. They were reassured and I agreed to carry out a review after four months.

PG: That's good to hear. What worried me, though, was that even with the support of the TA, some of those children seemed to take up an awful lot of the teacher's time. I'm sure the rest of the class must be getting a bit fed up about that. There are other children in the class who deserve more TA and teacher time but we're often told we can't afford it. It does seem a bit unfair on the ones that behave well.

CG: This does need very close monitoring, doesn't it? I mean, by the time the data comes out, it might be too late, if it shows the children's performance declining. There's always that lag, isn't there?

Head: Fair points, fair points. First, though, I am monitoring the classes affected pretty much daily, if I can. From what I've seen, things are getting better. At first the children needed a great deal of one-to-one support and there were some significant disruptions before they really settled down. We did anticipate that, though, and I can assure you that the teachers are not having to spend nearly as much time on the new children as they did at the beginning – and I fully expect things to go on improving.

PG: That's good to hear but I thought you said at an earlier meeting that we were having to supplement supporting their needs from the budget, so isn't that detracting from the education of the others?

Chair: We looked at that at Finance committee. Yes, we are redirecting some funding to support the children in the first couple of months but we expect that to drop off once they settle down.

PG: But how long is that going to continue? Our budget isn't looking great now and it's going to get worse next year. And if we take it away, won't the behaviour deteriorate?

CG: And I'd like to know whether, if the children don't integrate properly, I mean if they become really disruptive, would you consider excluding them? At what point do we say enough is enough?

Head: OK. Well, financially, the extra support from the school budget will be withdrawn from the beginning of next month. The extra funding from the LA will continue, of course, so I don't expect any major deterioration. And, yes, if the worse came to the worse – which I really don't think will happen, but if it did – yes, I would exclude if absolutely necessary.

Chair: I understand colleagues' concerns but there's a danger we lose sight of the main thing here. We all agreed to take on these children and give them a fair chance – and it seems to be working, as I understand it. We're nowhere near needing to exclude them and I don't see any reason to expect that we will need to do so. It's important that we show our support to the head and staff.

PG: Yes, fair enough. I agree that we should continue, as long as we get regular reports from the head.

CG: I don't want to appear churlish but I'm not quite so happy about the situation. I'm glad that we'll keep getting the regular reports but we can't afford to damage the chances of the majority just to make life better for a couple of the children, however much sympathy I might have for them. I worry that if we're not careful we'll just get used to worse behaviour and worse results.

Head: It is a difficult balance, of course. I'm not naïve or complacent. I agree that we can't afford for our results to get worse and I have no intention of allowing that to happen. But I do want us to do the best we can for all the children, not just the amenable ones with lots of support from home. Children, in my experience, are resilient and adaptable – more so than we sometimes give them credit for.

CG: OK. I'm sorry if I gave the impression that I thought you were complacent. I know you're not and I do think we should keep on with these children unless and until things take a turn for the worse.

Chair: I think that's probably as far as we can go with this at the moment. It will be a regular agenda item so we won't forget about it.

COMMENTARY

This vignette shows governors using questioning very effectively to test out the veracity of the head's actions and interpretation of what is happening in the school.

It illustrates a classic dilemma – balancing the needs of a few versus the needs of the many. The discussion arises from a governors' day in school, which reflects openness and a willingness to hear from the governors what they think might improve the school.

The headteacher appears to be open-minded but also clear thinking and willing to take hard decisions. He/she is monitoring the situation directly and believes that it is under control but, when pushed, says that he/she would exclude the new pupils if absolutely necessary.

The parent and co-opted governors present a series of challenging questions and follow-up questions and are not easily distracted from their enquiries, doing so strongly but respectfully. This is a good example of effective challenge.

The chair manages the discussion effectively by, for example, making clear very early in the discussion that "we're not going to talk about individual children or teachers" and using summarising as a way of refocusing and moving the conversation on.

The essential challenges revolve around: the school's values, especially in relation to inclusion; the support available; the needs of the majority of the class; the needs of the new children and parental concerns.

Having explored the issue reasonably thoroughly, the chair brings the discussion to a close with a commitment to continue monitoring the situation.

What could the chair and governors do next?
They will need to monitor the situation closely and persistently through committee and full governing body meetings, challenging regular reports from the head and staff on the matter. They will need to hold the head to account if the situation deteriorates and ensure that the head's assurances given in the meeting are realised over time.

Your thoughts, observations and ideas

Principles of Effective Challenge

Some common obstacles

Living in the community

Sometimes feelings can run high in schools, governing bodies and their communities. An unexpectedly bad Ofsted report or a proposed change of status, for example, can provoke strong debate and polarised views. Governors can easily be caught in the middle and run the risk of being shot by both sides. Parents may react badly and take out their feelings on the governors they know, either because they did or didn't ask the right questions.

In a less dramatic context, where the school may be doing well and parents are happy, a governor may choose not to ask the necessary question for fear of provoking a particular group of staff or parents who are their neighbours.

This potential restriction should not be underestimated. We should be brave as governors and follow Lord Nolan's principles of public life, but it is not always easy. (The Seven Principles of Public Life – the "Nolan Principles" – are on www.gov.uk/government/publications/the-7-principles-of-public-life.)

Fears of retribution

Similarly, governors may fear retribution from the head and/or staff if they are seen to be critical – particularly parent governors, who may fear it will be not so much aimed at themselves as at their children in the school. One would always hope that the professionals in school would never seek to take out their feelings on pupils but, sadly, it does sometimes happen. It can also be seen in comments to the governor's child from the children of the governor's neighbours, reflecting or echoing what their parents have said.

Managing risk

Governors might be tempted to avoid challenging the headteacher of a school getting consistently great results, even if areas like financial management might be less than squeaky-clean. Why rock the boat and risk the school's reputation?

Strategies for effective challenge

Get it right – ask the right question at the right time in the right forum of the right person in the right way

Effective challenge can depend on a lot of different and sometimes conflicting factors. The right question at the wrong time or in the wrong forum can lead to an unsatisfactory outcome. The right question asked in the wrong tone of voice can be counterproductive. The right question asked of the wrong person won't lead to the answer you need.

Don't underestimate yourselves

The quality of governance and the skills, experience and behaviours of governors have been rising steadily in recent years. The DfE's insistence on the importance of appropriate skills rather than representation as the main qualification for being a governor has had an impact. Many governors bring to the role high-level, sophisticated skills and abilities that can be applied very effectively in the school and governance context. Objectivity is vital.

Be clear about your motivation

Why do you wish to challenge the head? Is it in the best interests of the children? Make sure there's no personal agenda. If you dislike or disapprove of the head, and especially if this is known, it's probably best if someone else pursues the challenge so that it cannot be misinterpreted as a personal attack or vendetta.

Base it on objective evidence and use objective evidence to pursue it

What facts have you got at your disposal? Are you fully confident of the grounds of your challenge? If you anticipate a glib or superficial answer, have you prepared follow-up questions based on the same or further evidence? Can you access that data or evidence quickly and easily when you need it?

Don't give up after one question: be persistent but don't nag

It is often the third or fourth question that really gets at the truth. Professionals are good at answering initial and immediate follow-up questions. It's tempting to accept these responses but then later on realise that they don't really answer the question. Be prepared to ask a series of questions, but this must be balanced with awareness of the effect of persistent questioning on the head and others involved. If there are other important issues to be explored in a limited amount of time, it might be sensible to agree to move on but return to the topic on another occasion. If so, it is important to ask for this to be an agenda item and record this in the minutes as an action.

Seek allies and prepare
It is easier to pursue a challenge if you are confident that others are with you. It is dangerous to assume this rather than talking to colleagues in advance to find out where they stand on a particular issue. If you haven't been able to secure this support ahead of a meeting, then it may be crucial to read the mood of the meeting and the body language of colleagues to see if they are in support or not.

Preparation is vital
Do your research. Check the facts. Think about the timing of your questions. Phrase your questions with care. Make sure you have evidence to hand, if challenged yourself. Identify your allies.

Be firm and clear but not aggressive
Asking a well-crafted question is a sophisticated skill – the sort of thing that lawyers and police officers have to learn in order to succeed. Forensic questioning is well-targeted, carefully phrased and allows very little room for evasion. Politeness and respect are an important element of this. The more aggressive the questioning, the less likely it is that you will get to the truth. Don't confuse aggression with persistence and assertiveness. Be prepared to recognise the truth when you see it, even if it conflicts with any presuppositions. Be big enough to admit that you are wrong, when it's appropriate.

Know your rights
As we have seen, challenging (balanced with supporting) is absolutely central to the governor's role. It is more than legitimate – it is vital. Heads should expect it and see it as healthy – part of the process of improving the school.

Consider why you may not be getting the answers you need
Heads, like governors, are only human. Much depends on the quality of the relationship between governors and the head. If mutual trust and respect have been damaged or haven't had time to develop fully, then putting this right should be the top priority. Most people, when put under pressure, can behave defensively or seek to avoid the situation through a variety of deflecting actions, especially if and when weaknesses are exposed – or are in danger of being exposed. When people are tired or have had a particularly challenging day they are less likely to respond well to even well-meant and gentle questioning. Ask yourself whether there is a developing pattern of behaviour. Does the head often

become emotional when questioned? Does the head behave differently depending on who is asking the question? Understanding human behaviour is a lifelong task but most of us are reasonably skilled at seeing what lies beneath the surface. Being sensitive to the head's frame of mind and empathising with them is important but should not deter us from ever asking a tough question.

Don't store up unsatisfied challenges

If the head is evasive, vague, unresponsive or emotional when challenged, with the result that governors do not get satisfactory answers to their questions over a significant period of time, there can be a dangerous build-up of frustration that can suddenly explode, sometimes in response to an innocuous moment, causing hurt feelings and a poisoned atmosphere. This can be cathartic but might also be very damaging to individuals and the effective maintenance of a good working relationship between head and governors. Nipping this in the bud is the best way forward, but it does not always work at first or even after several attempts. A good chair will sense a developing problem and seek advice and peer support in addressing it before it becomes a crisis. However, even where all this has been tried, in some circumstances an early resolution just isn't possible and the volcano explodes.

Appoint a professional clerk

As the *Clerking Competency Framework* (DfE, April 2017) says: "Professional clerking plays a crucial role in supporting the board to hold executive leaders to account. It provides guidance to the chair and board to help them identify the information they require and the questions they should ask of senior leaders. It works with senior leaders to provide the information and data that the board requires about education standards and financial performance in a timely manner. This gives the board the opportunity for detailed scrutiny of data before discussions and facilitates challenge of executive leaders about current performance and strategic priorities. Professional clerking also informs the board's accountability to others through minutes that provide evidence of challenge and scrutiny of the executive, and the board's overall ability and capacity to govern the organisation well."

Seek external validation and advice

Because governors are not usually educational experts, they can lack confidence in identifying areas for legitimate challenge. Getting a second opinion from an expert can be very helpful but isn't always easy to achieve and may cost the school money. Nonetheless, this is less expensive than having the school go into special measures because the governors didn't notice what was going wrong.

Access training
Because the data and its interpretation can be complex and sophisticated, governors should not assume that they can simply wing it and just use their common sense in identifying areas for challenge. It is important for at least some of the governing board to undertake relevant training in order to boost the collective confidence of the board in raising legitimate questions. Other forms of training may also be available and helpful, such as how to balance support and challenge.

Talk to other governors from other schools
One important side benefit of attending governor training is meeting other governors from different schools and sharing problems and solutions. But this can be achieved in a variety of other ways, too, such as online and via social media. If you have only ever been a governor at one school, you may have no idea whether what your school does is normal. However, schools are remarkably different from each other and develop different cultures and practices over time. Finding out that other governors experience the same issues as you can be reassuring. Finding out that what your school does is very different from most others can be good, if the outcomes are brilliant, or worrying if not. Either way, you go away feeling wiser.

How do you know, as a board, whether you are challenging effectively?
It is not sufficient to wait for the next Ofsted inspection to find out whether the board is doing its job of challenging school leaders effectively or not – though it could happen at any time, of course.

The *Competency Framework for Governance* identifies some useful indicators, especially in section 2f, External Accountability. According to the Framework, "This section is about managing the organisation's relationship with those who have a formal or informal role in holding it to account. It enables the board to use their skills and knowledge confidently and effectively to be accountable for the delivery of the organisation's strategic plan, their own decision-making and their oversight of executive leaders."

It identifies the need for the following knowledge, skills and behaviours:

Everyone on the board

Knowledge

• the purpose, nature and processes of formal accountability and scrutiny (e.g. DfE, Ofsted, EFA etc.) and what is required by way of evidence

• the national performance measures used to monitor and report performance – including the minimum standards that trigger eligibility for intervention

Skills and effective behaviours

• ensures appropriate structures, processes and professional development are in place to support the demands of internal and external scrutiny

• values the ownership that parents and carers and other stakeholders feel about "their school" and ensures that the board makes itself accessible and answerable to them

• uses an understanding of relevant data and information to present verbal and written responses to external scrutiny (e.g. inspectors/RSCs/EFA)

The chair

Skills and effective behaviours

• is confident in providing strategic leadership to the board during periods of scrutiny

• ensures the board is aware of, and prepared for, formal external scrutiny.

While these expectations go a long way towards clarifying what is expected of governors, they do not provide a full answer. Regular self-evaluation, ideally facilitated or verified by an external adviser, should ensure that the board's challenge function is performed well.

Vignette 7
WINDFALL

Head: I'm pleased to say that the academy has £80,000 more than expected because the funding allocated for accruals hasn't been fully required. We were, as you know, holding back £50,000 for CIF projects which are not going ahead. That's a disappointment, of course, but we can now go ahead with some refurbishment.

Chair: So what's most in need of refurbishment?

SBM: Well, there are four main areas. The Evans Block needs repainting and rewiring and all the windows need replacing. So that's one obvious priority. The school kitchen really needs a major overhaul, maybe £8,000 for the structure and about £12,000 to install the kitchen. Beyond that, the lunchtime area also needs brightening up and making more attractive to the students. If there's anything left after those improvements, then the sixth form area could do with a face lift, especially by the time we're recruiting later this year.

PG: Why have those particular items had been selected as priority areas?

Head: The Evans Block is 50 years old now and needs more than a cosmetic change. The conditions for learning are really sub-standard. We have been trying to promote better health generally and especially healthy eating, so improving the catering facilities is essential. Again, the kitchen equipment is beyond the normal replacement date. We want to improve take-up of the sixth form and we can't pretend that cosmetic aspects don't play a part in encouraging students to stay and attracting new ones.

PG: If we did all that, would it use up all of the £80,000 you mentioned?

Head: Yes, it would, but let's not forget that we're in the very fortunate position of having reserves of over £400,000. That's much more than many schools I know. Quite a few have deficit budgets now.

Chair: So what does that mean? Are we holding back a lot more than we should? What's the average size of a school's reserves? I mean, in schools like ours?

SBM: Our current policy, based on what our accountants advise, means we should hold £500,000 in reserves.

PG: So what's that based on?

SBM: How do you mean?

PG: Well, is there some common formula or something? What does Ofsted say about it?

Head: If I'm honest, I'd have to say that there's not really a scientific approach to calculating that number but it's equivalent to about four to six weeks of expenditure. Ofsted don't really have an official view but they tend to go along with that advice. If we were retaining too much, they would challenge us.

Chair: So what are the reserves for, then?

Head: Essentially, it's a contingency fund, to ensure we don't run out of cash for salaries, mainly, in the short term.

Chair: We know that every month we get about £330,000 from the EFA so why do we need reserves?

PG: I understood from the finance training I did that reserves should be linked to Risk Register items. What are the school's major financial risks?

Chair: What's the argument for reducing the reserve?

Head: That's a lot of questions at once! Let me try to clarify matters. It's essential that any refurbishment is in line with the priorities in the improvement plan and the strategic plan. The changes we're proposing are all intended, ultimately, to improve things for the students and enhance their progress and performance over time. We have to think about opportunity costs, too. Spending money on enhancements now will reduce the risk of the Evans Building being condemned, for example, which would cost an astronomical sum to replace entirely. But, at the same time, capital spending of £50,000 may not be enough. If capital expenditure were increased to, say, £100,000 a year we could make a series of improvements to increase the value of our assets rather than allowing a decline.

PG: That makes sense, I agree. But what about the sixth form spending? That building's pretty much OK, isn't it? We had a meeting there about a month ago and it looked fine to me.

Head: Yes, you're right. It's not in dire need but at the same time it is deteriorating and certainly needs more than a lick of paint. Our long-term strategy is to grow the sixth form, which will bring in more income, so it's a virtuous circle. But 16+ students have a lot of choice in this area and our rivals are spending all they can afford to boost their numbers, so we can't afford not to, in my view.

Chair: There's a lot there to think about. I think it would help us if by the time we meet again, we could consider a more detailed proposal for increasing capital expenditure to £100,000 for the next three years. Would that be do-able?

Head: I think so. What do you think?

SBM: Yes, it shouldn't be a problem.

COMMENTARY

This vignette shows how a lack of training and strategic planning can undermine governors' ability to challenge.

It is unusual for a school to have a surplus budget but there are some that do. The issue here is about what to spend the money on.

It is slightly odd that there should be a debate about this at this stage. One might have expected the head and governors to have drawn up a plan prioritising areas of need before this moment.

The governors are presented by a small range of options by the SBM, which might well be perfectly reasonable, but it seems to come as news to them. The parent governor asks right away: "Why have those particular items had been selected as priority areas?" A very good question!

The head provides a rationale which then leads to a series of challenging questions from the governors, led by the chair. Whilst the questions are well focused, they betray a level of ignorance that could be worrying ("What's the average size of a school's reserves? I mean, in schools like ours?"). One might expect a chair to be better informed. Also, the advice given during the meeting is that the recommended reserve is £500,000 yet the governors are discussing digging into an amount of only £400,000.

The debate becomes animated as the governors start to explore the reasons for a school holding a reserve. The head is bombarded with questions, not least from the chair. On paper, the head's answers seem reasonable and clear but what's lacking is any consideration of alternative spending options.

The chair rounds things off somewhat abruptly but also pragmatically. The governors need more information before endorsing the head's and SBM's proposals, so the request for a more detailed proposal for increasing capital expenditure makes sense. However, it is not clear whether the governors have approved the proposals for spending the windfall or not, which is a very unsatisfactory result.

While the governors clearly offered clear challenge, it did not lead to a definitive outcome.

What could the chair and governors do next?

It may be that they realise after the event, especially when they read the minutes, that the matter was not resolved satisfactorily, and they return to the issue at the earliest opportunity. Although one of the governors referred in the meeting to having attended finance training, there seems to be a general lack of understanding of how academy finance works, so there is a need for more governors, especially the chair, to undertake training. They will also need to make sure that the head and SBM present the governors with the detailed proposal within the agreed timescale.

Your thoughts, observations and ideas

Challenge in Particular Contexts

The small village school

Small village schools are often popular and successful, and achieve great outcomes for the pupils – but not always. They are vulnerable to a range of challenges, including fluctuating pupil numbers and budget, wider demographic changes, curriculum breadth and teacher expertise, and a very heavy workload for staff, especially the headteacher.

Each year group will be small and therefore each pupil represents a high percentage of the cohort. If the previous cohort contained no pupils with SEND and the current Year 6 has a number of children with significant special educational needs, then it might be reasonable to expect a drop in outcomes. But this can easily become a self-fulfilling prophecy. Governors need to be particularly assiduous in monitoring the progress of all pupils in this cohort throughout their time in the school, especially those with SEND.

Children with challenging behaviour can have a disproportionate effect on a small school, but then again, the family atmosphere can be just what the child needs. A school unused to coping with such children can misjudge the level of challenge being presented.

The family atmosphere can make it harder for governors to present effective challenge, especially if relationships become too cosy over time and they get lured into being more operational than strategic.

Remaining objective is one of the keys to success in this context. Benchmarking your school's performance is a useful safeguard against any argument that your little school is unique and cannot really be compared to any other. There are, in fact, many small – even tiny– schools around the country. Meeting governors from other similar schools can also provide a helpful perspective.

The outstanding school

If your school was graded outstanding by Ofsted in the last two or three years, the chances are it will still be outstanding. The more time passes, however, the more that outstanding status could be under threat, not least because Ofsted's definition of outstanding can and does change over time, usually becoming more demanding. In theory, if a school is deemed to be outstanding, it will not be inspected again unless there is factual evidence of a drop in standards.

On 6 January 2017 *Schools Week* reported: "The latest official statistics from Ofsted show that 106 schools have gone more than 10 years without a full inspection; 372 are recorded as not receiving one since 2007; 398 since 2008; and 407 since 2009. In total 1,283 schools appear not to have been inspected for more than seven years."

Those that have not been inspected for the longest time tend to be the outstanding schools since even good schools are usually re-inspected after about three years, albeit only for a short inspection. In practice, however, a series of triggers could precipitate an earlier visit by the inspectors.

It is also possible for outstanding schools to fall into the category of "coasting", if complacency sets in, which can happen quite easily.

The governors in outstanding schools are faced with some tough but not insurmountable problems. Total perfection is seldom universal even in an outstanding school. They should check that all pupils and students are achieving their full potential, especially focusing on the relative performance of the groups of children that Ofsted look at : children with English as an Additional Language, for example, and, especially, children eligible for the Pupil Premium. They can also look at all the other areas of school performance mentioned earlier, such as safeguarding, behaviour and finance.

However, there are some dangers in this. If they continue to challenge when academic outcomes are as good as they can get, they risk alienating their leadership team, who could well respond by saying "What else do you expect us to do?" If they start looking at other aspects of the school to improve, they could be accused of nit-picking. They have to be eagle-eyed to spot any decline emerging through data analysis.

On the other hand, Ofsted has, from time to time, downgraded schools overnight from outstanding to inadequate, often to the amazement of the governors who had no idea that things had deteriorated so drastically – or, more likely, didn't notice because they were too complacent.

The Requires Improvement school
While it's not a comfortable situation to be in, when your school is deemed by Ofsted to require improvement, governors are usually in a strong position to insist on and facilitate change. After all, the school's strengths and weaknesses have been identified by external experts who will have included in their report a clear set of requirements to improve

it, so the governors' agenda is already determined and the parents are well aware of what needs to change and why. In addition, the governors may well find help coming their way from either the local authority or the academy trust. Ofsted will keep up the pressure through regular monitoring visits, all within a clear timetable for improvement.

What could possibly go wrong?

It may be that some or all of the governors – and possibly some staff and parents – are in denial about the need for change, so their reluctance to accept the judgements and move on can be an obstacle to improvement and slow it down.

Governors can feel overwhelmed, especially if the judgement came as a shock. They can also be overwhelmed by too much unco-ordinated support from other agencies. They can feel terrorised by the urgency of the change agenda and schedule. They may find that the demands on their time and commitment are excessive, far greater than they are used to.

But at the same time, they should find that effective challenge is modelled for them by experts and the culture change required is a revelation, empowering them in new ways. Finally, they understand the role and how to carry it out well.

The quality of governance may itself be questioned and Ofsted may have recommended an external review of governance, designed to highlight strengths and areas for improvement. Even if this has not been mentioned, it would be good practice for the governors to undertake such a self-evaluation, ideally facilitated by an external expert. Governors should always be open to challenging themselves.

The academy within a Multi-Academy Trust

Some multi-academy trusts have chosen to remove local governing bodies from individual academies, replacing them with more distant and collective governance.

Where a local governing body (LGB) exists, its terms of reference should be defined clearly in a scheme of delegation. Often the LGB's main purpose is to provide accountability, especially in relation to the school's standards, which would involve all the common aspects of challenge. This can feel akin to the role of a Curriculum and Standards committee of a maintained school governing body. Its core aims can be very achievable because of a lack of distraction caused by a wider range of responsibilities and compliance factors such as finance, strategy and human resources, leaving the LGB free to focus on standards. It can also, though, leave the governors feeling emasculated, with too many aspects of the school beyond their control and influence.It can be particularly frustrating to have little or no control over the school budget, since potentially it takes achieving the school's aims out of your control.

Much depends, then, on the degree of autonomy, power and responsibility delegated to the LGB and its relationship to the trust board. The governor in an LGB needs to be very clear about the level of delegated responsibility in order to both not overstep the mark but also be confident in fulfilling a legitimate role.

The challenge role in this context will normally be enhanced by the work of the trust board in ensuring high standards across all its academies.

The special school

Special schools are both the same as and different from other schools. They are the same in the sense that the "normal rules" apply to them and, like other schools, their governing bodies have to manage the curriculum, staffing, premises, safeguarding , etc – and governors can and should offer challenge in relation to all these areas, as appropriate. They are different in the sense that they teach children and young people with a range of special educational needs, including disability and behavioural issues. Some special schools cater for children with moderate learning difficulties (MLD) while others focus on severe learning difficulties (SLD).

So, for governors of a special school, on the one hand all the areas covered in the *Governance Handbook* apply to them but, on the other, understanding the curriculum offered and judging the progress and attainment of pupils is more complicated.

While every "mainstream" school has been getting to grips with "assessment without levels" and adopting new approaches to judge the standards achieved by their young people, special schools have been doing the same. The extra difficulty they face is that the attainment of many, if not most, of their pupils could not be measured by the old National Curriculum levels, so they referred to a range of pre-national curriculum levels known as "P" levels. But at the time of writing, P levels look likely to be abolished, following a national consultation process. The usual benchmarking data sets are not much use to the special school governor since they are based on assessment systems used in mainstream education.

In relation to a fully inclusive approach to assessment, the final report from the Commission on Assessment without Levels (DfE, September 2015) said:

"Assessment needs to be holistic and consider long term wider outcomes such as higher education, employment and independent living. Schools should consider meaningful ways of measuring all aspects of progress including communication, social skills, physical development and independence. Assessment should reflect the extent to which a pupil can apply their learning in a wider range of contexts and enable teachers to determine what they need to do to ensure that the intervention and support provided enable children to progress in all areas of their learning and development. High expectations should apply equally to pupils with SEN and disabilities as to all other pupils. For many pupils with SEN and disabilities effort applied to learning is significant and assessment should recognise this alongside outcomes achieved whilst maintaining high aspirations and expectations. For pupils working below national expected levels of attainment assessment arrangements must consider progress relative to starting points and take this into account, alongside the nature of pupils' learning difficulties."

So governors of special schools need to know what assessment systems their school is using, how they work and what data is collected, and to make sure this data is shared with them regularly. It can be argued that these governors, more so than those in more mainstream schools, need to see the outcomes of regular specialist external evaluations of the school in order to be confident that their school is getting it right.

Balancing Challenge with Support

When asked why they became a governor many, if not most, governors say that it's because they want to "give something back" and support their school. They tend not to say, "Because I want to challenge and hold the headteacher to account."

This is to be welcomed, of course, as long as they learn quickly that support alone is not what is required.

Challenge is defined reasonably clearly, as we have seen, especially by Ofsted and the DfE but that is not so true of support. It is easy to offer the wrong kind of support and for schools sometimes to expect it. Understanding the governance role – by staff and governors alike – is essential to getting it right.

Governance is essentially a strategic role, not an operational one. Offering support can easily be misinterpreted as meaning "lending a hand" and governors can find themselves running stalls at the school summer fete or digging a new garden for the pupils to grow plants. These are not evil or forbidden acts: they are just not governance.

Does this mean that governors should never be operational? Not necessarily, though it does depend a little on one's understanding of "operational". A governing body that never sees the school in action during the day is unlikely to make better decisions than one that remains aloof, meeting only once the children and staff have left. Drawing up policies and never seeing directly the extent to which they are followed in practice can lead to a shelf full of dusty, unused folders of meaningless documents. The school's ethos can be written down as a series of aspirations, but what matters is the consistency of their application and realisation, which is best experienced first-hand.

There can be times when being operational is essential. This is from the *Governance Handbook*: "Since the board is responsible in law for the school, it may need to intervene in operational matters if a circumstance arises where, because of the actions or inactions of executive leaders, the school may be in breach of a duty. Having advised the board, executive leaders must comply with any reasonable direction given by it."

Support, as with challenging and holding to account, cannot be done on the basis of data analysis alone: we need to see for ourselves what the school is like, what it is like for teachers and pupils. Reports can help

71

but the evidence of one's own eyes can provide a living, breathing context for the numbers on the spreadsheet.

Purposeful support

The *Governance Handbook* provides a useful structure for consideration of how we can best support our school, especially in the form of the six features of effective governance:

1. Strategic leadership that sets and champions vision, ethos and strategy

2. Accountability that drives up educational standards and financial performance

3. People with the right skills, experience, qualities and capacity

4. Structures that reinforce clearly defined roles and responsibilities

5. Compliance with statutory and contractual requirements

6. Evaluation to monitor and improve the quality and impact of governance.

This book has focused very much on the second feature on the list, accountability, but the remaining five are equally important and all, implicitly, offer areas in which the governors can support the school. The final four features, especially, point to ways we can be supportive in a purposeful way and are linked by a focus on improving our efficiency and effectiveness as individuals and as a governing board. In other words, the best way we can support our school is by being good at what we are there to do.

There are ways we can support the school by not doing certain things, such as not getting involved in day-to-day school management issues and not making unnecessary demands of school leaders.

Here are some practical ways we can support our school:

- championing the school in the local community
- acting as a sounding board for senior school leaders, especially by the chair
- praising and rewarding significant staff achievements
- lobbying on behalf of the school, e.g. for additional resources
- being visible in school, e.g. attending assemblies/performances
- suggesting evidence to support school's self-evaluation judgements
- showing concern for staff well-being

- dealing effectively with parental complaints
- participating in staff selection processes, where appropriate
- responding meaningfully to School Council proposals
- conducting staff exit interviews
- being consistent and resolute in supporting staff and pupil disciplinary issues
- encouraging the school to look outwards and forwards.

Vignette 8

A HEALTH AND SAFETY ISSUE

Chair: Which brings us to Health and Safety. Sally, I think you wanted to review the recent incident in terms of lessons learned?

Sally (PG): Thanks, Gina. Yes. Well, I don't want to go over the whole thing in detail again because we've had the report and it's pretty clear what happened. It's more about making sure we're confident it couldn't happen again. In a nutshell, a few weeks ago, one of the dinner ladies, Mrs Carrington, found a syringe lying in the playground. She picked it up and handed it in to the office. As far as we can be sure, no child touched it or went near it. The site manager did a full search after break ended and didn't find anything else. The head asked him and Mrs Carrington to write a report each and the deputy head wrote it up. We discussed it at our last meeting, as you will have seen from the minutes. Basically, we're happy that it was a one-off and unlikely to happen again. No one was injured. As you all know, some parents got the wrong end of the stick and started a discussion on Facebook, alleging that drug users were regularly breaking into the school site at night and leaving drug paraphernalia lying around which any child could pick up. The local newspaper picked up the story and published a lurid version of events without checking any of the details with the school before publication.

New governor (Hanif): I think some of this happened before I joined the governing board. I have read the report but I'm hazy about some of the details. For example, how did the syringe get there?

Sally: We don't know. We think it was probably chucked over the fence by someone.

NG: Was it used? I mean, was there any drug residue in it? It must have been a possible infection risk if a kid had picked it up.

Chair: I'm not sure about that. The important thing was that an adult found it and dealt with it.

NG: Did she wear gloves or use a tissue?

Chair: I think she folded down her sleeve and picked it up like that.

NG: And when she handed it in, did the office staff handle it safely? Did Mrs Carrington clear the playground as soon as she found the syringe?

Sally: Well, no, because it was near the end of break and most of the children were in the main part of the playground, away from the wall.

Head: There were weaknesses in the way the incident was dealt with and we are seeking to learn from anything that went wrong in order to improve our practice. Hanif, I know that you have some experience from your professional background in dealing with this sort of incident and we would welcome any insights you could provide. However, I think it would be best if we have that detailed discussion outside this meeting as our time is somewhat limited. I don't want to shut down discussion but now is not the time and place. The draft report is still very much up for amendment.

NG: OK, that seems fair. How about if I re-read the report and put my thoughts in writing?

Head: That would be great. Thanks, Hanif. I'll need them by the end of next week, though, if that's possible?

NG: That shouldn't be a problem. So, at the start Sally said we need to make sure it couldn't happen again. Could you go over what actions have been taken to achieve that, please?

Head: The chair and I wrote to the local paper expressing our disappointment about the lack of professionalism from the paper with very little fact checking, including the background and motivations of the small group of parents who discussed the issue on Facebook. We are taking legal advice about this. Obviously, we don't deny that all secondary schools have some issues with drugs but we feel it has been exaggerated in this case. We have reviewed our safeguarding policies. Teaching about substance abuse is part of PSHE and is also covered in other areas like assemblies and one-to-one interventions. We have also asked for outside advice from a local drug prevention body. This group has met and reviewed our PSHE component on substance abuse. They were satisfied with the approach the school is taking for drugs education and have asked to see the materials used in order to assess this further. They have also offered to run workshops and to take direct referrals.

Chair: That's really good to hear. What about the parents, though, and the police?

Head: We offered the parents writing on Facebook the chance to meet with senior staff to discuss any issues. They haven't taken up the offer, I'm afraid. We have liaised with the police and they have assured us that there have been no reports about regular drug use in this part of town, so it does seem to have been a one-off.

Chair: Well, pending Hanif's critique of the draft report, I think it's fair to say that we're satisfied with the school's response both to safeguarding and substance abuse education. Agreed? OK, thanks. So, as there is no evidence of drug taking on the premises, there seems to be no further action for us to take, other than to continue to monitor the robustness and effectiveness of the policies.

COMMENTARY

This vignette shows the value and, simultaneously, the danger of intense, forensic questioning – but it is managed effectively by the chair.

Sally's summary of events lists a series of issues that need to be addressed, but it seems that this has happened and the purpose of the discussion is to make sure everyone's confident it couldn't happen again.

New governor Hanif homes in on some very specific details about the original incident, displaying some careful and intelligent questioning – though it risks getting the governors bogged down in the fine detail which has probably already been explored. Sally and the chair are probably not the best people to be answering these questions since they don't seem to have been directly involved at the time of the incident.

The head skilfully picks up on this, reminding everyone of the purpose of the discussion, acknowledging Hanif's specialist knowledge and seeking to utilise it in an appropriate way. Hanif's response is constructive and helps move the discussion on. The head's account of the actions taken by the school in response to what happened seems detailed and thorough. The chair asks specifically about the parents and the police and receives reassurances from the head. The governors appear to be satisfied with the head's account, as long as Hanif's critique doesn't undermine it.

What could the chair and governors do next?

The chair and head will need to make sure Hanif does what he has agreed to do within the timescale set. There will be a need for a further discussion, probably at committee level, about Hanif's critique, and actions agreed, if necessary.

Your thoughts, observations and ideas

Conclusion

In his foreword to the *Governance Handbook*, Lord Nash writes: "I want everyone involved in governance to be confident in tackling underperformance, challenging mediocrity, and setting the highest of expectations; refusing to accept second best for any child."

The DfE and Ofsted quite rightly have high expectations of school governors when it comes to challenge, but while they offer some pointers as to how this can best be achieved, they offer few, if any practical suggestions that acknowledge the formidable complexity and variety of the current schools system, let alone the very real human relationship and behavioural issues that can either facilitate or block effective challenge.

This book has attempted to explore some of that complexity, present some possible strategies and offer insights into some very specific scenarios in which governors attempt to offer challenge.

It isn't possible to consider and explore every possible context in such a short space. But I hope that readers can apply some of the lessons outlined to their own particular situation and find their own way of challenging the professionals in a productive way that ultimately benefits the young people in our schools.

If, having read this book, you are left feeling that your governing body is not up to the challenge of challenging, take heart from this extract from *Improving Governance: Governance arrangements in complex and challenging circumstances* (Ofsted, 2016):

"There were common challenges … governors did not have enough focus on raising standards and school improvement. They did not make effective use of information about pupils' performance. Many governors were unable to account for the impact of additional funding to support disadvantaged pupils. However … it is possible for weak governance to improve quickly. Neither the types of school nor the structure of governance were the reasons for the original weaknesses in governance. There were three critical factors that made improvements possible:

- the schools became aware of the weaknesses in their governance arrangements

- they were able to develop professional knowledge, understanding

and insight within the governing board
- establishing clarity about governors' roles, responsibilities and lines of accountability"

The book started with one of my favourite quotations, which is applicable in many situations: "There are three sides to every story: yours … mine … and the truth. No one is lying." It captures the subtlety of the problem of challenge: no one is lying because we all tend to believe our own perspective on events and evidence and we may believe our truth passionately, which can blind us to others' truths.

Acknowledging the validity of alternative versions of "the truth" and seeking to understand them could be the beginning of wisdom.